Mediterranean Diet Italian Edition

Achieve Vibrant Health Through Mediterranean Recipes From the Italian Coast

DevelopedLife.com

Photo Credit:

The cover of this book includes a photo of beautiful Positano, Italy taken by Flickr user Eric Hossinger, who donated the picture for public use.

See More At:
https://www.flickr.com/photos/hozinja/with/6188223020/

Developed Life Books
4884 W. Hardy Rd
Tucson, AZ 85704
US

First Printing – 2016

Introduction

Thank you a lot for buying this book! I hope it will assist you on your healthy journey into Mediterranean eating. After you've done trying out these delicious recipes, please remember that a review on Amazon would really help me to keep going with all this.

Get My Books For Free!

If you bought this on Kindle for a couple of dollars (or on paperback for a few more) I greatly appreciate it. However, keep in mind you also have a chance to receive some of my products for free. This is by signing up to my mailing list. I will periodically run a free promotional tool, and I'll let my subscribers know whenever I do this.

In addition, everybody who signs up receives a FREE copy of my book: **The 20 Most Deceptive Health Foods**

The point of this book is to educate readers about what foods are actually healthy, and which ones are not.

It's a must-have to take with you to the grocery aisles.

You can join the exclusive mailing list right now at the following link:

http://www.developedlife.com/andreasilver.

This is my completely free gift for my subscribers.

A Note About Measurements

I generally create these recipes using all or part of the metric system. This is more handy for exact measurements. There are many sites like metric-conversions.org where you can do conversions if you're not sure how to use metric or if you don't have a scale. If you are from the UK or USA and you are confused at all, go to this exact address: http://www.metric-conversions.org/volume/milliliters-to-us-cups.htm (this is for ml to US cups, as an example simply switch to UK cups or a different measurement that fits your country).

Through using ml this way for any type of recipe, you get exact amounts versus approximations.

Getting Started With Mediterranean Eating

Today, the Mediterranean diet is quickly becoming one of the most popular diets, and for good reason: studies have shown the longevity of people from all across the coastlines of countries like Greece, Italy, Cyprus, Turkey, and other regional countries.

The reason is because of the abundance of fresh ingredients, healthy fats in the form of oils, omega acids, and plenty of greens—both cooked and raw—to provide alkalinity and more health effects.

There's been a lot of fad diets. The reason the Mediterranean diet especially appeals to me is because there's no funny research, marketing, or sketchy pseudo-science from less-than-reputable journals that get inflated on daytime TV. It's a no-brainer that relates to how people in other cultures live their lives by contrast to our own.

This is also why nutritionists point out that eating like somebody living in the Mediterranean does not involve just following recipes with a sense of superiority. Rather, as with any diet, it involves more of a lifestyle change. This may include:

Being more European in your commute habits: In many of the countries which this diet applies to, people stay mobile. They walk to work, walk to the grocer, or walk to their neighbor's houses. If you live in a region like the United States, most of us spend all of our time in-between the couch (Netflix), the car (commuting), and the office chair (working).

This, of course, means you are spending most of your time in a sedentary way. The alternative is to get a gym membership, but these rarely last because the gym is not integrated holistically into how you lead your life. It becomes a stressful event of going from non-physical activity to suddenly strenuous physical activity. And this is why people burn-out and don't maintain their health resolutions.

Integrating physical activity into your life is one of the key reasons why in many parts of the Europe, there is simply not the abundance of overweight people like you see in North America. So ask yourself how you can apply this to your life. It may even involve keeping your car in the garage and figuring out what errands you can accomplish on foot.

Eating local: I remember when I first started to really pay attention to the ingredients labels in what I was buying; I was aghast to discover that a lot of the bread at a supermarket in Phoenix, AZ contained additives like high fructose corn syrup.

The reason you'll find added sugar for example in commercial foods is because they are committed to one thing: the bottom line. If your bread is in competition with a different bread company, and you need to stand out and increase sales, what do you do? Well, one idea is to make your bread more addicting and sweet. So, just dump some corn syrup into it and problem solved!

The same thing occurs in fast food. Recently, McDonalds had to deal with decreasing sales of their Egg McMuffins. Their solution was: add butter. Sure enough, their sales bounced back.

Traveling to the Mediterranean, I discovered something surprising: there are far fewer commercial versions of necessities like bread and dairy. Even major commercial chains seemed to be stocked with locally produced merchandise. And even those brands which were packaged elsewhere did *not* contain corn syrup or other additives.

The reason is two-fold: Europeans prefer their local products, as they've been eating them for centuries, and Europe generally has stricter regulations. Many European countries will not allow artificial dyes, artificial sweeteners that are proven as toxic, GMO foods of a dubious origin, or the adding of corn syrup or excess sodium to try to hook people on a particular product.

So, if you're not from a culture that is savvy in this way, what can you do? The answer is to shop a bit smarter. Even if you prefer to shop at major, commercial food grocers—you can still find 'local' food at the grocer's bakery. Instead of buying a loaf of pre-sliced bread, go to the bakery and buy a freshly baked loaf and slice it yourself.

Or, you can start going to farmer's markets. These are sometimes harder to find—and more expensive, but it's almost always worth it. Some people swear by shopping like this, and I can perfectly understand why. Which leads to my next point:

Be dairy smart: The sign of a healthy egg is if you break the yolk, and it's a dark, golden yellow color. The majority of eggs we buy come from inhumane conditions, where chickens are stuffed into cramped conditions their whole lives, jabbed full of antibiotics and hormones, and forced to produce eggs en masse. You'll find typical commercial eggs, when you crack them, the yolks are an unhealthy pale color.

If you buy actual farm-raised eggs, you'll find the yolks look the healthy way they're supposed to. During my months touring the Mediterranean, **almost every egg yolk I broke looked proper**. This says a great deal about both the conditions of the chickens, and also the nutritional qualities of what's being eaten.

As a non-vegan (who respects vegan diets), I do think if I'm going to eat dairy, it should be higher quality. I can guarantee these parts of the world eat better dairy than what North Americans in particular are used to.

Socialize more: Finally, did you know a diet may involve non-food related activities? Mental health is a huge part of physical fitness. Stress alone is a major component of weight gain (not to mention depression). I personally think it's more than possible to lose weight simply through increasing your R&R time and socialization opportunities.

I can't give you exact directions on how to do this. However, it's just something to keep in mind. Ask yourself what steps you can take in your life to begin spending more time around friends and family (at least those ones who you enjoy spending time with).

A Few Frequent Questions

Before we dig in, I thought I'd address a couple of common questions first.

What about drinking wine?

Wine is considered a part of the Mediterranean diet. Good luck keeping your average Greek or Italian away from his or her wine for more than a day or two. This is a bit different if you're focusing on Middle Eastern Mediterranean regions, like Turkey, where large parts of the culture are dry due to Islamic cultural traditions.

That being said, despite the health benefits of wine (resveratrol, the powerful antioxidant), alcohol is still a vice to be regulated. Long-term alcohol consumption increases both weight gain, and the odds of acquiring diseases, including cancer. This is why a glass of wine every couple of days shouldn't morph into a bottle of wine once a night. There's never any reason to delve into alcoholism!

What about pasta?

Mediterranean diets are not as pasta-heavy as you think. It's best to avoid excess pasta usage in any recipe, and when possible substitute white-pasta for whole-grain pastas.

All white-pastas, or white-carbs in general, are heavy sugar producers. This doesn't mean you should avoid it at all costs, but understand that it definitely doesn't help if your goal is weight-loss. Simple carbohydrates cause blood-sugar spikes. Your body immediately starts eating your glucose, storing the rest away in glycogen deposits. Excess glucose is stored as fat. Long-story short, simple carbs promote weight-gain and imbalanced sugar-levels.

What about sugar?

If you lead a healthy, active lifestyle, you can handle a bit of sugar if a particular Mediterranean recipe calls for some honey, for instance.

I have very little patience for our addiction to artificial sweeteners. If a recipe calls for honey or sugar, I'd put it in. Don't substitute it with chemicals just to get the sweet fix.

Alternatively, don't eat sweet foods all of the time. You shouldn't be eating so much sweet things that you feel it's necessary to start adding artificial sweeteners to compensate.

However, a tablespoon of honey now and then, I guarantee, won't harm you.

The Italian Side of the Mediterranean Diet

As I began researching Mediterranean recipes, I found something surprising: there was a lack of Italian-style dishes; yet there was a never-ending supply of Greek recipes. I think this is because traditionally, Mediterranean recipes skew towards Greek staples like hummus and yogurt. Italian food, which is more focused around pastas, often flies under the radar of those committed to healthy lifestyles.

Italy shares a coast with the Mediterranean all along the southern sides of the peninsula, and Italian cuisine can be nicely integrated into a Mediterranean diet; with all of the same (or more) health benefits of Grecian-influenced food.

One common complaint about Italian cooking is that it focuses too much on simple-carbohydrates in the form of white-pastas. This can be easily alleviated by eating whole-grain pastas, or substituting pasta for a vegan alternative, such as "zoodles" (zucchini-strip pasta). I'll incorporate some of these recipes in this book.

Some of the healthiest Italian recipes includes the many varieties of antipastos; filled with olives, artichoke hearts, and other nutritious ingredients. Recipes loaded with peppers contain carotenoids, vitamin C, and many other nutritious properties. The soups in this book have super-food ingredients like kale, and the entrees—including the non-vegetarian ones with meat—are balanced with fresh garden ingredients to ensure you're getting the most from your diet.

Let's go on to the recipe now!

Appetizers

Artichoke Tortillas

Quick to make, delicious and really healthy!

Ingredients

- 4 tortillas. I prefer wheat or grain to cut back on the simple carbs.
- 3 tbsp olive oil
- 1.3 kg of spinach leaves
- 170 g of garlic and herb goat cheese
- 340 g of marinated heart artichokes, drained and chopped
- 1 tomato, chopped
- Salt and pepper

Directions

- For each tortilla, brush both sides with olive oil and grill in the oven on medium heat for a few minutes. On each grilled tortilla, spread some cheese and top with spinach leaves, artichokes and tomato. Season with salt and pepper.

- Place the tortillas back into the oven for 2 mins until browned.

Serves: 4

Caprese Pesto with Chives

Chive-pesto is a delicious Mediterranean / Italian specialty.

Ingredients

- 2 flat breads
- 8 cherry tomatoes
- 125g Nonfat mozzarella, thinly sliced

Pesto:

- 16 g of chives
- Some basil leaves
- 40 g of pine nuts
- 20 g grated parmesan
- 1 garlic clove, crushed
- ½ a lemon juice
- 118 ml of olive oil

Directions

- Preheat your oven to 200 degree celsius and cut your tomatoes.

- On each flatbread, spread some of the pesto sauce and top with two slices of mozzarella and tomatoes.

- Bake in the preheated oven until crispy for about 10 mins.

- **To make the pesto sauce:** Simply blend all the ingredients together. You can make it easier with a food processor.

Serves: 2

Zucchini Pesto Mini Buns

These "sliders" taste great with homemade pesto. Make an extra portion of the pesto and keep it around for other sandwiches.

Ingredients

- Whole wheat mini buns, cut in half, toasted
- 2 zucchini, thinly sliced
- olive oil
- Pinch of salt and pepper
- 6 cherry tomatoes, halved
- Green olives, halved

For the pesto:

- 20 g basil leaves
- 1 small clove of garlic, crushed
- 2 tbsp part-skim ricotta
- 1 tbsp olive oil
- 1 tbsp parmesan cheese, grated
- Pinch of kosher salt
- Pinch of grounded black pepper

Directions

- **To make the pesto:** Blend the basil, garlic and olive oil in a food processor. Blend in the ricotta, parmesan, salt and pepper.

- In a pan, heat 1 tsp of olive oil and cook the zucchini slices in batches on medium heat. Season with salt and pepper and flip the sides.

- On each bun, arrange the zucchini slices on the bottom and top with pesto , tomato and olives. Sprinkle with pepper and tp with basil leaves. **Serves: 2**

Sicilian Style Crackers

Ingredients

- Whole wheat crackers
- 12 red bell peppers
- 400 g kalamata olives , pitted and chopped
- 4 tbsp olive oil
- black pepper

Directions

- Roast the pepper in the oven with the rest of the ingredients,

- Cool and blend the roasted vegetables. Spread some of the paste on crackers and top with slices of tomato.

  Serves: 2

Mini Zucchini Pizza

Ingredients

- 1 tbsp olive oil
- 3 zucchini, cut in circles
- Salt and pepper
- 118 ml marinara sauce
- 50 g Nonfat mozzarella, thinly sliced
- 25 g of cubed tomatoes
- 1 tbsp Italian seasoning

Directions

- Preheat oven to 200 degrees Celsius.

- In a pan heat the olive oil, and cook the zucchini circles on each side until golden. Season with salt and pepper. Transfer the circles onto a baking sheet and arrange in a single layer. Top each circle with some marinara, aslice of mozzarella and tomato.

- Bake in the hot oven for 3 mins, transfer to a serving plate and sprinkle with seasoning.

Serves: 2

Pesto Pasta Salad

Ingredients

- 800 g cooked whole wheat fusilli pasta
- 149 g cherry tomatoes, halved
- 1 carrot. cubed
- 8-10 asparagus (blanched and diced)
- 90 g olives sliced
- 90 g capers
- 110 g feta cheese
- 25 g sun dried tomatoes
- 30 g baby spinach leaves cleaned
- 2tbsp pepper
- 350 ml of pesto (a good store bought brand or make your own from one of the above recipes)
- 20 g pine nuts
- Salt

Directions

- In a large bowl, toss the cold pasta with the pesto. Add salt and pepper.

- Add in the rest of the ingredients and toss to combine.

Serves: 4

Sicilian Eggplant Caponata

Caponata is a famous, delicious Italian-Mediterranean hors d'oeuvres. This recipe involves a mix of caponata with eggplant and avocado.

Ingredients

- 2 tbsp capers, drained
- 60 ml olive oil
- ½ kg eggplant, peeled and diced
- 1 onion, chopped
- 1 celery rib, chopped
- 1 tomato chopped
- 2 tbsp red wine vinegar
- 2 tsp sugar
- 1 tsp pine nuts
- Salt and freshly ground pepper
- 1 avocado, diced

Directions

- In a pan, heat 3 tbsp of the olive oil and add the eggplants and cook on high heat on both sides for 10 mins.

- Transfer the eggplant to a bowl.

- In the pan, add the rest of the olive oil and add the onion and celery, cover and cook for 10 mins. Then add the tomato, cover and cook for 5 extra mins.

- In a saucepan, add the vinegar with the sugar and allow to simmer until sugar dissolves. Add in the pine nuts and capers and cook for a minute.

- Back to the pan, return the eggplants in the pan and add the vinegar sauce with it and cook for 4 mins. Season with salt and pepper and transfer to a serving bowl. Add the avocado and toss to combine.

Serves: 2

Antipasto Bocconcini with Olive Tapenade

Ingredients

- 3 tbsp green-olive tapenade
- 1/4 cup pepperoncini, stemmed, seeded and chopped
- 118 ml olive oil
- 225 g bocconcini (or you can use nonfat mozzarella)
- 1 tbsp + 1 tsp fresh lemon juice
- 1 tbsp + 1 tsp red wine vinegar
- 1 tbsp + 1 tsp garlic, garlic
- 1 tsp dried oregano
- Salt
- Freshly ground pepper
- 1 small watercress, shredded
- 6 small basil leaves
- 90 g green olives

Directions:

- In a bowl, mix together the tapenade with the pepperoncini with 59 ml of olive oil. Then add the bocconcini and toss to combine.

- In a bowl, whisk together the vinegar, lemon juice, garlic and the oregano. Whisk in the remaining oil and season with salt and pepper.

- In a bowl, combine the watercress and the marinated bocconcini and half of the dressing and toss to combine. Transfer to serving plate and top with basil and olives and drizzle the dressing around the salad

Serves: 8

Grape Salad

Ingredients

- 65 g chopped pecans
- 225 g organic whole wheat farfalle pasta
- 550 g broccoli florets, finely chopped
- 220 g plain Greek yogurt
- 50 g sugar
- ¼ 55 ml red wine vinegar
- 1/2 red onion, diced
- ½ tsp salt
- 200 g seedless red grapes, halved

Directions

- Preheat oven to 176 degrees Celsius and roast the pecans on a baking sheet for 7 mins.

- Cook the pasta according to the instructions on the package and drain. Mix together the yogurt, sugar, vinegar, onion and salt.

- In a large bowl, combine the pasta with the broccoli and grapes and toss to combine and gradually add the yoghurt mixture. Refrigerate for 3 hours.

- When ready to serve, toss the toasted pecans and serve.

Serves: 6

Light Mozzarella Tomato Salad

Use the freshest ingredients you can find.

Ingredients

- Kosher salt
- 1 kg summer tomatoes, bottoms crossed with a knife
- 100 g small black olives, pitted
- 2 tbsp capers, rinsed
- 16 g torn basil leaves
- 2 tbsp balsamic vinegar
- 59 ml extra virgin olive oil
- Black pepper, freshly grounded
- 0.2 kg mozzarella
- 20 g of arugula leaves

Directions

- In a pot on high heat, bring water to a boil and add salt. Prepare a separate bowl of ice water and place aside.

- Drop the tomatoes into the pot of boiling water for 10 seconds and remove from the water and drop into the ice water. Slip off the skins and remove the cores. Chop the tomatoes and add the olives, capers, vinegar and oil. Season with salt and pepper. Transfer to serving plate.

- Cut the mozzarella into 3 pieces and arrange them on top of the salad. Sprinkle with arugula.

Serves: 6

Asparagus and Scallion Salad

Ingredients

- 0.6 kg fresh asparagus, shaved, cooked, sliced (1 inch)
  0.3 kg scallions, trimmed, sliced (1 inch)
  1 tsp salt
  3½ tbsp extra-virgin olive oil
  1½ tbsp red wine vinegar
  Salt and pepper
- 3 hard-cooked eggs, peeled, cut in wedges and sliced

Directions

- In a pot, boil one quart of water and poach the vegetables for 6 mins and season with salt. Drain on kitchen towel.

- Pile the sliced asparagus and scallions and drizzle oil and vinegar on them. Sprinkle with salt and pepper and toss well to combine.

- In a bowl, toss together the eggs and vegetables, add more oil and vinegar as a dressing if necessary, and transfer to serving plate.

Serves: 4

Quick Pasta Salad

Ingredients

- 375 g whole wheat rotini pasta, cooked, drained
- 125 g feta cheese
- 150g cucumber, diced
- 200 g black olives, sliced
- 2 tsp Italian salad dressing
- 50 g sun-dried tomato, chopped

Directions

- In a large bowl, combine the cooked pasta with the cucumber, olives, tomato and feta. Toss to combine.
- Season with salt, pepper and Italian seasoning and fridge for two hours. Serve.
- Optionally drizzle some olive oil / and or vinegar on it.

Serves: 4

Antipasto Salad

Ingredients

Dressing

- 6 tbsp extra virgin olive oil
- 59 ml red wine vinegar
- 1 clove garlic, crushed
- 1 tsp mustard
- ½ tsp sugar
- ½ tsp salt
- ¼ tsp black pepper

Salad

- 272 g watercress, chopped
- 200 g roasted red peppers, sliced
- 170 g artichoke hearts marinated in oil, chopped
- ½ an onion thinly sliced
- 16 g parsley leaves
- 100 g Kalamata olives, pitted, halved
- 50 g shredded mozzarella
- 100 g organic chery tomatoes, quartered
- Pepperoncini peppers

Directions

- Prepare the dressing, by whisking all the ingredients very well.

- In a large bowl, toss together the watercress, peppers, artichoke hearts, red onion, parsley, olives, mozzarella and tomatoes.

- Drizzle the dressing over the salad and toss well to combine.

Serves: 6

Colorful Salad

Ingredients

Dressing:

- 118 ml extra-virgin olive oil
- 2 tbsp honey
- 2 tbsp white vinegar
- 1 clove garlic, crushed
- 1/2 tsp Italian seasoning
- 35 g Parmesan cheese, grated
- Sea salt and black pepper

Salad:

- 50 g finely diced red onion
- 100 g artichoke hearts, chopped
- 100 g diced plum tomatoes, pitted
- 100 g cucumber, cubed
- 25 g sun-dried tomato, chopped c
- 50 g feta cheese
- 100 g black olives, sliced
- 200 g chickpeas, drained
- 200 g whole grain penne pasta, cooked
- 272 g watercress, chopped
- Sea salt and black pepper
- Red pepper flakes

Directions
- First make the dressing by blending all the ingredients except the salt and pepper. Then after blending the ingredients, season with the salt and pepper. Place the dressing in the fridge until ready to serve.

- For the salad, toss everything together, except the watercress, pepper and red pepper flakes, in a large bowl.

- When it's time to serve. Place the salad in serving bowl and drizzle with the dressing. Toss to combine. Season with salt and pepper and garnish with red pepper flakes.

Serves: 6

Mediterranean Caprese

Dressing

- 118 ml extra virgin olive oil
- 59 ml vinegar
- 2 tbsp water
- 1 tsp Garlic and Herb seasoning
- 1 tsp honey
- 1 tsp lemon zest
- Pinch of salt

Salad

- 170 g mozzarella
- 184 g marinated artichoke hearts
- 100 g black olives, pitted
- 170 g grape tomatoes
- 2 tsp Garlic & Herb Seasoning

- Make the dressing by blending the ingredients together.

- Make the salad by chopping the mozzarella into small chunks and place in a bowl. Add in the olives, artichokes, tomatoes, seasoning and pour ¾ of the dressing and toss to combine.

- Refrigerate until ready to serve.

   Serves: 5

Marinated Artichoke Heart Salad

Ingredients

- 4 small zucchini, sliced in semi-circle, steamed, drained
- 175 g large black olives, pitted, drained
- 175 g marinated artichoke hearts, drained
- 1 green pepper, chopped
- 1 red onion, chopped

Dressing
- 236 ml sugar-free olive oil and vinegar dressing
- 2 tbsp lemon juice
- 20 g grated Parmesan
- 1 tbsp dried pesto
- 1 tsp dried oregano

Directions

- Mix together the zucchini, olives, artichoke hearts, pepper and onion in a jar and pour in the dressing over, close the jar and shake to combine. Refrigerate for 8 hours

- Marinate in refrigerator 4-8 hours. Drain and transfer to serving plate and top with a little bit of grated parmesan.

Serves: 4

Roasted Pepper and Goat Cheese Salad

Ingredients

- 2 large red bell peppers, oven roasted
- 2 large yellow bell peppers, oven roasted
- 10 Sicilian green olives, cracked
- 6 oil-packed anchovy fillets, chopped
- 2 tbsp capers, drained
- 1 tsp rosemary, chopped
- 1 tbsp red vinegar
- 2 tbsp olive oil, plus more for drizzling
- Six 1-inch-thick slices of whole grain peasant bread
- 1 large garlic clove, crushed
- 200 g low fat goat cheese, cut into 12 pieces

Directions

- Chop your roasted peppers into strips after removing the seeds.

- In a large bowl, combine the anchovy, capers, rosemary, vinegar and 2 tbsp of oil and add in the peppers.

- Rub each bread slice with some oil and vinegar and grill the bread in the oven until crispy and browned.

- In a serving plate, arrange the goat cheese and the grilled bread slices next to it and serve with the salad.

Serves: 6

Insalata Mediterranea

A type of tossed Italian salad.

Ingredients

- 2 heads romaine lettuce, chopped
- 80 g purple onion, sliced
- 168 g artichoke hearts, drained, chopped
- 134 g olives
- 2 medium tomatoes, sliced in wedges
- 1 cucumber, sliced
- 1 red pepper, sliced
- 100 g feta cheese, crumbled
- Italian salad dressing
- 2 tbsp apple cider vinegar
- 1/4 tsp onion powder
- 1/4 tsp garlic powder
- 1/4 tsp paprika
- 1/4 tsp sea salt
- 1/2 tsp Italian herbs
- Pinch black pepper
- olive oil

Directions

- In a large bowl combine the all the ingredients together apart from the Feta, and season according to your taste. Place in serving plates and top each serving with some crumbled Feta.

Serves: 6

Crockpot Italian Quinoa Soup

If you don't have your own crockpot, you can just use a large, normal covered pot and it should still be OK. This is a side-soup but it could also be a meal in itself.

Ingredients

- 2 small chicken breasts, boneless, skinless
- 1 cup onion, chopped
- 1 cup celery, chopped
- 1 cup carrots, diced
- 3 tbsp olive oil
- 1 1/2 teaspoon garlic, minced
- 140 g uncooked quinoa
- Tomatoes, oven roasted, diced
- 1/4th a liter of chicken broth
- 1/4 tsp red pepper flakes
- 1 tsp Italian seasoning
- 2 tsp dried oregano
- 1 full tbsp dried basil
- Salt and pepper
- Parmesan Cheese
- Fresh parsley, to garnish

- In a pot, add the olive oil, chicken, onion, celery, carrots, garlic, quinoa, tomato on low heat. Then pour in the broth and add the seasonings.

- Cover and cook on very low heat for 2 hours. Shred the chicken and return to the pot and adjust seasoning.

- Shred the chicken and return it to the crockpot. Add in any more seasonings to taste. Pour in serving bowls and garnish with parsley.
  Top each bowl with freshly shredded Parmesan cheese and enjoy! **Serves: 6**

Ribollita

This famous soup recipe has its origins in Tuscany. It's a hearty farmer's stew designed with the working class of old in mind. It's highly nutritious, especially with the inclusion of kale.

Ingredients

- 1 onion, chopped
- 2 carrots, chopped
- 1 tomato, chopped
- 1 zucchini, chopped
- 4 garlic cloves, crushed
- 1 bunch kale, stems removed, roughly chopped
- 1 handful parsley, roughly chopped
- 2 tbsp olive oil
- A pinch dried red chili flakes
- 10 sage leaves
- 300 g cannellini beans
- 0.9 ltr vegetable stock
- Kosher salt and black pepper
- Wholegrain sourdough bread, oven toasted, cubed
- Parmesan cheese

Directions

- In a large pan, heat 2 tbsp of oil and add the garlic, onion, carrots, chili and sage leaves, and cook on low heat for about 20 mins. Add in the parsley, tomato, zucchini and cook for a few more minutes, stirring regularly.

- Next, add in the beans and the kale and pour in the stock. Bring the soup to a boil and reduce the heat and let it simmer for half an hour. Season with salt and pepper.

- Pour the soup into serving bowls and top each serving with some bread toasted cubes and sprinkle some parmesan cheese and a drizzle of olive oil.

Serves: 2

Cheesy Green Bean Bake

Ingredients

- 30 ml olive oil
- 0.68 kg French green beans, ends cut off, rinsed, chopped
- 11/2 tsp crushed garlic
  Salt
  Black pepper
- 2 tbsp grated parmesan cheese
- 150 ml grated mozzarella cheese

Directions

- In a pot of boiling water, cook your beans for 10 mins.

- In a pan, heat 15 ml of the olive oil and cook the garlic in it.
  Add the remaining oil and add in the beans and stir. Season with
  salt and pepper and transfer to a shallow baking dish. Sprinkle
  with parmesan and mozzarella and bake in the oven for 20 mins.
  Serve warm.

  Serves: 8

Simple Shrimps

Ingredients

- 1 garlic clove, crushed
- 2 tbsp olive oil
- ½ tsp salt
- ½ tsp oregano
- 0.5 kg cooked medium shrimps, thawed
- 60 ml olive-oil based Italian dressing

Directions

- In a pan on medium heat, heat the olive oil, add the garlic and cook for a minute. Add the shrimp and arrange in a single layer in the pan.

- Transfer to a bowl and add the Italian dressing and toss to combine.

- Place in serving plates and serve with steamed broccoli.

  Serves: 1

Spring Soup

A soup of fresh greens. Highly nutritious.

Ingredients

- 1 tbsp olive oil
- 1 tbsp margarine
- 1 large leek , thinly sliced
- 1.8 liters of low-sodium vegetable stock
- 113 g whole grain pasta
- 226 g sugar snap peas, halved diagonally
- 340 g broccoli rapini, chopped
- 6 spring carrots, diagonally cut

Directions

- In a pan over medium heat, add the oil and margarine and mix together. Once the margarine is melted and foams are visible, add the leeks and cook for 3 mins.

- In a pot over medium-high heat, pour in the vegetable stock and bring to a boil. Add the rest of the ingredients into the pot along with the leeks and let it cook for 20 mins.

Serves: 4

Hearty Macaroni Stew

Maybe you've had the canned-version of macaroni soup before. This, however, is the real thing. Elbow-shaped pasta has been around since before Campbell's Soup made it popular.

Ingredients

- 2 tsp olive oil
- 1 small onion, chopped
- 2 garlic cloves, crushed
- 1 tomato, chopped
- 950 ml reduced-sodium vegetable broth
- 237 ml water
- 2 red potatoes, chopped in 1 inch chunks
- 65 g elbow macaroni
- 280 g of frozen cut green beans
- 439 g red kidney beans, drained
- 170 g baby spinach
- 30 g grated Parmesan cheese

Directions

- In a pot over medium heat, heat the oil and add the onion and garlic and cook for 3 mins. Pour in the broth and add the water, potatoes, and pasta.

- Bring soups to a boil and reduce the heat and allow it to simmer for 7 mins, covered. Make sure the vegetables are cooked. Add the beans and spinach. Cook for 3 more mins and transfer to serving bowls. Top serving with a sprinkle of grated parmesan cheese.

Serves: 4

Italian Garden Soup

Another wide assortment of vegetables turned into a tasty soup. This recipe is vegan.

Ingredients

- 3 tbsp olive oil
- 4 large carrots, sliced
- ½ bunch of celery, chopped
- 2 onions, chopped
- 4 cloves of garlic, crushed
- 2 large peppers (different colors)
- 1 head of broccoli, chopped
- 4 large tomatoes, chopped
- 75 g fresh mushrooms, sliced
- 411 g fire roasted organic tomato, diced
- 425 g corn, drained
- 250 g frozen peas
- 200 g cups fresh beans
- 3 potatoes, diced
- 2 litres water
- 3 tbsp tomato paste
- 3 large bay leaves
- 10 g dried basil
- 1 tbsp sea salt
- 1/2 tsp black pepper
- 1/4 tsp crushed red pepper flakes

Directions

- In a pot over medium heat, heat the oil and add the vegetables and cook while stirring.

- Pour in the water once the vegetables are cooked and then add tomato pasta, bay, basil, salt, pepper and the red pepper flakes.

Cover and cook for 2 hours, constantly checking. Turn off the heat and stir, season with more salt and pepper and serve warm.

Serves: 4

Classic Chicken Vegetable

Ingredients

- 1 onion, chopped
- 2 stalks celery, chopped
- 1 carrot, chopped
- 1 tbsp oil
- 3 cloves garlic, crushed
- 0.95 liters chicken stock
- cauliflower
- cabbage, chopped
- chard, chopped
- red bell pepper, chopped
- green beans
- celery root, chopped
- 237 ml chicken meat, cooked, chopped
- 85 grams salsa
- 1/8 tsp black pepper
- 11 grams herbs such as (oregano, thyme, tarragon, parsley)
- oregano

Directions

- Cook the onion, celery, and carrot in the pot for 2 mins, and then add the garlic and chicken.

- When the soup boils, check seasoning, add more water if needed.

- Add in the salsa, black pepper and herbs and turn off the heat and serve warm.

Serves: 4

No-Cook Soup

Here's one for the raw-foodies.

Ingredients

- 1 fresh tomato
- ½ fresh cucumber
- ½ celery stalk
- 93 g rice flakes (or oat flakes)
- 2 tbsp pumpkin seed flour
- about 1 cup hot or cold water or vegetable broth
- 1 tbsp olive oil
- ½ tbsp soy sauce
- Spices: salt, black pepper, dry garlic, dry porcini mushrooms, smoked paprika, cayenne pepper, Italian spice
- 15 g chopped spinach leaves
- 1 tsp barley grass powder
- ½ tsp spirulina

Directions

- In a food processor, blend the tomato, cucumber, celery and rice flakes. Then add in the pumpkin flour, olive oil, soy sauce and the spices and blend again.

- Then add the spinach, barley grass powder and spirulina and blend again until smooth.

- Serve with a dollop of plain yogurt, or if you're vegan—forget that last suggestion.

Serves: 4

Main Courses

Mediterranean Pizza-Style Skillet

Olives, fresh feta, chicken, artichoke hearts, basil—this is a very tasty dish that encapsulates the essence of the Italian coast.

Ingredients

- 3 medium chicken breasts halves, cut ¾ pieces
- 2 gloves of garlic, crushed
- 2 tbsp olive oil
- 4 tomatoes, chopped
- 240 g artichoke hearts
- 64 g olives, pitted sliced
- ½ tsp dried Italian seasoning
- Pinch of pepper
- 150 g lettuce, chopped
- 110 g Feta, crumpled
- 8 g basil leaves, torn
- Oven-dried whole-wheat French-bread slices

Directions

- In a pan over medium heat, cook the chicken in the olive oil and garlic until browned and add in the tomato, artichoke, olives, seasoning and pepper

- When the mixture boils, lower the heat and cook for 10 more minutes and add in the lettuce and cheese. Transfer to serving bowl and serve with slices of crispy bread.

Serves: 4

Crusted Chicken Piccata

Ingredients

- 25 g flour
- 2 eggs
- 125 g grated Parmigiano Reggiano cheese
- 1 boneless, skinless chicken breasts, halved and pounded 1/4-inch thick
- Salt
- 226 g whole grain angel hair pasta
- 3 tbsp extra virgin olive oil
- Juice of 1 lemon, plus 1 sliced lemon
- 2 cloves garlic, minced
- 25 g capers, drained and patted dry
- 118 ml dry white wine vinegar
- 8 g parsley, chopped
- 118 ml chicken stock
- 2 tbsp butter, cut into small pieces
- 141 g baby spinach
- Pepper

Directions

- In a bowl, beat the eggs. In another bowl place the flour. In another bowl place the cheese. Dip and coat the chicken in the three plates in the order of: flour, egg then cheese. Arrange on a plate.

- In a pot, bring water to a boil, add salt and cook the pasta according to the instructions. Drain.

- In a large pan, heat 2 tbsp of oil and add the chicken and cook until deeply golden on both sides for 10 mins. Transfer to a platter and cover with foil. In the pan, add the remaining oil and add the sliced lemon, garlic and capers and cook for a few minutes. Mix in the vinegar and parsley and stir. Lower the heat and bring to a simmer.

- Pour in the chicken stock and in the butter and lemon juice, and spoon some over the chicken. Add the spinach and cook until it wilts. Add the pasta and the cooking water and season with salt and pepper. Add in the remaining cheese and toss to combine.

- Serve with the pasta.

Serves: 4

Mediterranean Salmon

This Italian-style salmon dish includes pesto and is a great combination of different healthy ingredients.

Ingredients

- 0.3 kg salmon, or two large filets
- 1 tbsp pesto
- 2 tbsp sundried tomatoes
- 25 g red onion, minced
- 25 g feta cheese crumbles
- 10 Kalamata olives, pitted, chopped

Directions

- Heat the oven to 175 degree Celsius and line a baking sheet with parchment.

- Rub each salmon with pesto and place on the baking sheet. Arrange the feta, red onion, sundried tomatoes and olives on top of the salmon.

- Bake for 30 mins. Serve warm.

Serves: 2

Mediterranean Toss

Ingredients

- 2 tbsp olive oil
- 2 small zucchini, sliced
- 10 small sweet bell peppers, sliced
- 100 g cherry tomatoes, halved
- ½ yellow onion, diced
- 2 cloves garlic, sliced
- 1 tbsp dried Italian seasoning
- 1 tsp salt
- 425 g artichoke hearts in water, drained, halved
- 30 g sun-dried tomatoes in oil
- 80 ml balsamic vinegar
- 150 g dry whole wheat penne
- 25 g feta cheese, crumbled

Directions

- In a large pan over medium heat, heat the oil and add the onion, garlic, zucchini, peppers, tomatoes and cook until tender.

- In a pot, bring water to a boil and cook the pasta according to the instructions on the package. Drain.

- Add the Italian herbs, artichokes and sundried tomatoes to the vegetable mix and stir. Add the balsamic vinegar and mix.

- As the vinegar is reduced while you stir, add the pasta and toss to combine.

- Transfer to serving plates and top each serving with crumbles of Feta cheese.

Baked Rigatoni

Ingredients

- For the pasta:
- ½ kg whole wheat rigatoni
- 600 g heirloom tomatoes, chopped
- 118 ml water
- 70 g parmesan, shredded
- 5 tbsp pesto

Directions

- First cook your pasta according to the instructions on the package and preheat your oven to 200 degree Celsius.

- In a large bowl, toss together the cooked, pasta, tomatoes, pesto and some water. Transfer to the baking dish and sprinkle with cheese. Cover and bake for 15 mins.

Serves: 4

Eggs in Purgatory

Ingredients

- 5 small low-fat vegan sausage, cooked, chopped
- 50 g zucchini, diced
- 25 g minced onion
- 30 g red bell pepper, diced
- 2 cloves garlic, crushed
- 354 ml tomato puree
- 2 fresh basil leaves, torn
- 1 tbsp olive oil
- Pinch of dried oregano
- ¼ tsp sea salt
- ¼ tsp pepper
- 5 eggs
- 1 tbsp Italian parsley, chopped

Directions

- In a large pan over medium heat, heat the olive and add the onion, garlic and peppers. Stir and cook for 5 mins. Add in the zucchini and sausages and cook for 5 more mins.

- Add in the tomato sauce, basil, oregano, salt and pepper and stir. Cook for 5 more mins and when it starts to boil, reduce the heat.

- Make some space in 4 corners and one in the center of the pan and crack an egg in each space. Cover and cook on low heat for 12 mins.

- Top with parsley and serve.

Serves: 5

Sicilian Caponata

Ingredients

- 1 kg eggplant, peeled, chopped in ½ inch pieces
- 1 tbsp sea salt
- 118 ml extra-virgin olive oil
- 3 bay leaves
- ½ kg onions, chopped
- ½ kg celery, sliced 1/2 inch thick
- ½ kg cherry tomatoes, halved
- 20 g capers, well rinsed
- 20 large green olives, pitted chopped
- 2 fresh hot red chili peppers, seeded, halved, sliced
- 118 ml red-wine vinegar
- 1 tbsp honey
- 2 tbsp parsley, chopped
- 2 tbsp fresh basil, chopped

Directions

- In a large bowl, combine the eggplant and salt, transfer to a colander and set it to drain for an hour.

- In a large pan over medium heat, heat 59 ml of olive oil and add the bay leaves and cook for a minute. Add in the onions and celery and lower the heat and with regular stirring. Add the tomatoes, capers and increase the heat and cook for 5 mins. Add the olives and transfer to a large bowl.

- Rinse your eggplants and dry. Heat the remaining oil in the pan and cook the eggplants and peppers, while stirring for 10 mins. Transfer to the tomato mix and stir to combine.

- In a saucepan, whisk the vinegar and honey over medium heat and allow it to simmer. When it is reduced, add in the vegetables along with the parsley and stir. Serve warm. **Serves: 10**

Light Spinach Lasagna

A lower-fat alternative to Spinach lasagna. Just substitute for low-fat cheeses. Overall a very health entrée.

Ingredients

- 2 tbsp olive oil
- 1 tbsp minced garlic
- 2 tbsp minced fresh thyme
- 2 kg fresh spinach
- 900 g non-fat ricotta
- 1 egg
- ½ tsp salt
- ¼ tsp nutmeg
- 1 tbsp lemon juice
- 680 g lasagna noodles
- 2 cups non-fat mozzarella cheese, shredded

Directions

- Preheat the oven to 220 degree Celsius.

- In a large pan over medium heat, heat the oil and add the garlic and thyme and cook for 3 mins. Add the spinach and cook until wilted then remove from the heat.

- In a bowl, combine the ricotta, egg, salt, nutmeg, lemon juice and stir. Add in the spinach and stir. You can blend the mixture to get a smoother texture.

- In your cooking dish, spread some of the tomato sauce in the bottom of the dish. Layer 3 lasagna noodles and distribute the spinach mix into each layer evenly. Cover and bake for 40 mins. Remove the foil and bake for 10 more mins. Cool for 10 mins and serve. **Serves 12**

Italian Quinoa

Quinoa is really an all-purpose wonder-food. Here's an Italian-Mediterranean style spin you can cook up.

Ingredients

- 113 g eggplant, cubed
- 453 g tomatoes, cored, diced
- 1 tbsp extra virgin olive oil
- 1 medium onion, diced
- 4 cloves garlic, minced
- 124 g quinoa, rinsed, drained
- 500 g zucchini, sliced into rounds
- 1 can cannellini or navy beans, drained
- 1/2 tsp oregano
- Pinch of cayenne pepper (adds spice)
- 20 g fresh basil, chopped
- 2 tbsp fresh lemon juice
- Salt and pepper
- Chopped basil
- Grated parmesan

Directions

- Sprinkle the cubed eggplants with salt and place in a colander and let it drain for 20 mins. Rinse and dry.

- Blend the tomatoes in a food processor. In a pan over medium heat, heat the oil and add the onion and garlic and cook for 2 mins. Add the eggplants, tomato and about 60 ml of water. Stir and lower the heat and allow it to simmer for 15 mins.

- In a pot, boil around 237 ml—or 1 cup— of water and cook the quinoa.

- In the eggplant mix, add the zucchini, beans, oregano, pepper and 3 tbsp of basil. Stir and allow it to simmer on low heat and cook for 15 mins.

- Fluff the cooked quinoa with a fork and add to it the basil, lemon juice and salt. Stir and place aside.

- When the vegetable mix is forming into a sauce and there is less liquid, turn off the heat and season with salt and pepper.

- In each serving plate, put some quinoa and top with some of the vegetable mix. Sprinkle some parmesan cheese and garnish with basil.

Serves: 4

Braised Chicken

Ingredients

- 1 tbsp olive oil
- 4 whole chicken legs, skinned and cut into thighs and drumsticks
- 1 medium yellow onion, diced
- 3 carrots, diced
- 2 garlic cloves, crushed
- 2 tbsp fresh ginger, finely chopped
- 236 ml low-sodium chicken broth
- 236 ml water
- 200 ml dry white wine vinegar
- 4 sprigs thyme
- 25 g raisins
- 50 g large green olives, pitted. chopped
- 200 g chickpeas, rinsed and drained

Directions

- Preheat oven to 220 degrees Celsius

- In a large pan, heat the oil and add the chicken pieces and cook until crispy and golden. Transfer to a plate and place aside.

- Using the same pan but lowering the heat, add the onion, carrots, garlic and ginger. Add the broth, water, vinegar and bring to a boil. Return the chicken into the pan and add the thyme. Cover and bring to a boil and transfer to the oven. Braise for 45 mins.

- Remove from the oven and add the raisins, olives and chickpeas. Return to the oven and braise uncovered.

- Remove skillet from oven, and stir in raisins, olives, and chickpeas. Return to oven; continue braising, uncovered for 20 more mins discard the thyme. Serve hot.

Serves: 4

Mediterranean Style Pizza

Ingredients
- 1 prepared pizza dough
- 250 g artichokes hearts, sliced
- 50 g black olives, halved
- 1/2 small red onion, thinly sliced
- 1 tomato, thinly sliced
- 100 g chickpeas, cooked
- 90 ml pizza sauce
- Pinch of red pepper flakes, optional
- 7 large basil leaves
- Parmesan, grated

Directions

- Preheat oven to 170 degrees Celsius and place baking sheets inside it to heat. On a floured surface roll out the dough to form a thin pizza crust and place on the hot baking sheets and bake for 10 mins.

- Take the dough out of the oven and spread some sauce on each pizza, and layer the tomato, olives, chickpeas and red onion. Sprinkle red pepper flakes and salt. Bake for another 10 mins.

- Take the pizza out of the oven and top with basil and cut into slices. Sprinkle some parmesan and serve hot.

Serves: 6

Pizza Pasta

Pizza-style toppings in a pasta mix. Trust me, it's good!

Ingredients

- 226 g whole grain pasta
- ½ green pepper, diced
- ½ red pepper, diced
- 200 g cherry tomatoes, quartered
- 200 g mozzarella, diced
- ½ cup red onion
- ½ cup black olives
- 25 g parmesan cheese, grated
- 2 tbsp fresh basil
- 236 ml Italian dressing

Directions

- Cook pasta according to the instructions on the package.

- Toss together the cooked pasta, peppers, tomatoes, mozzarella, onion, olives. Pour in the dressing and toss to combine.

- Refrigerate for an hour. Transfer to serving bowl and top with basil and parmesan.

Serving: 2

Cauliflower Crust Pizza

Ingredients

- 1 small head cauliflower, cut into small florets
- 1 organic egg, beaten
- 50 g mozzarella cheese, shredded
- ½ tsp fine grain sea salt
- ½ tsp dried oregano
- ¼ tsp ground black pepper

Topping

- 75 g mozzarella cheese, shredded
- 113 g cooked spinach
- 50 g Pecorino Romano cheese, grated
- Handful sun-dried tomatoes, chopped

Directions

- Preheat oven to 220°C and prepare a baking sheet and grease it with olive oil.

- In a food processor, blend the florets and then microwave for 8 mins until cooked. Place the florets in a tea towel and squeeze the moisture out.

- Transfer the squeezed cauliflower in a bowl and add the egg, mozzarella, oregano, salt and pepper and mix well together.

- Now, press the mixture on a baking sheet into a pizza circle and bake for 15 mins, then take it out and let it set for 5 mins.

- Sprinkle the mozzarella over the pizza base and spread the spinach and Pecorino and add a pinch of salt. Put back into the oven and bake for 10 more mins.

Zoodle Bake

A "zoodle" is a healthy pasta alternative consisting of noodle-like zucchini shavings. Here's a great healthy Italian "zoodle" recipe.

Ingredients

- 4 zucchini
- 5 tbsp olive oil
- 1 tbsp dried basil
- 1 tsp dried oregano
- 1 tsp dried parsley
- 1/2 tsp red pepper flakes
- 1/2 tsp ground black pepper
- 2 tsp sea salt
- 60 ml black olives, halved
- 37 grams sun-dried tomatoes in oil, chopped
- 340 grams Nonfat mozzarella cheese, shredded
- 3 red bell, sliced
- 4 tbsp parmesan cheese, grated

Directions

- Preheat oven to 190°. Using a spiralizer or a sharp grater, shave zucchini spaghetti.

- In a large colander, toss the zoodles with 2 tsp of salt and place aside for 10 mins. Later, squeeze the zoodles by wrapping them in a tea towel and squeezing the liquid out.

- In a baking dish, add oil, basil, parsley, oregano, red pepper flakes, black pepper and the zoodles. Add in the olives and tomatoes. Toss well to combine. Drizzle with some olive oil and sprinkle ¾ of the mozzarella and red peppers. Then sprinkle the rest of the mozzarella and parmesan on top.

- Bake in the hot oven for 45 mins until browned, Serve warm.

Serves: 6

Shrimp Squash

Ingredients

- 59 ml olive oil
- ½ tbsp red pepper flakes
- 1 kg raw shrimp
- 50 g onion, chopped
- 500 g crushed tomatoes
- 2 tbsp garlic, minced
- 1 tsp dried oregano
- 1 large spaghetti squash, rinsed and pierced with a knife
- 1 tsp olive oil
- salt and pepper to taste
- 2 tbsp parsley, chopped

Directions

- Place your squash in the microwave and cook for 25 mins. Cool for 10 mins and cut in half and remove the seeds and scrape out the strands. Place in a large bowl and toss with the oil, salt and pepper.

- In a pan over medium heat, heat the oil and toss in the red pepper flakes then the shrimps. Cook for a few minutes. Remove and set aside in a bowl.

- In the pan. Place the onion and cook until tender, add the garlic and cook for a minute. Pour in the tomato, season with oregano, salt and pepper. Allow it to simmer for 20 mins.

- Now assemble the dish, spoon a quarter of the sauce into a deep serving bowl and top with squash. Top with shrimp and some parsley.

Serves: 6

Shrimp Scampi

Ingredients

- 4 zucchini, tops and bottoms cut off
- 0.5 kg raw shrimp- peeled, deveined
- 3 tbsp coconut oil can
- 1 medium head of garlic, diced
- Black pepper
- Parmesan, grated

Directions

- In a pan, heat the oil and add garlic and stir. Add the zucchini and shrimp, season with salt and pepper and increase the heat to high. Cook until the shrimp is pink. Transfer to serving plate, and top with parmesan. Serve hot.

Serves: 2

Fresh Zoodle Spaghetti

It's yummy and vegan

Ingredients

- 6 zucchini
- 5 links uncooked low fat vegan sausage, chopped
- 400 g cherry tomato halves
- 6 tbsp + 2 tbsp extra-virgin olive oil
- 1 tbsp minced fresh garlic
- 1 tsp. red pepper flakes
- 1 tbsp oregano
- 3 tbsp fresh basil, chopped
- 3 tbsp chopped flat, chopped
- Freshly grated Parmesan cheese, to garnish

Directions

- In a pan over medium heat, heat 1 tbsp of oil and cook the vegan sausage, break it up using a potato masher. Using a spiralizer, shave zucchini noodles. Add the garlic, red pepper flakes and the tomatoes and cook for 5 mins.

- Remove the sausage from the pan and set aside, and add 6 tbsp of oil into the pan and heat for a minute. Add in the sausage, oregano, basil, parsley and cook for 5 more mins.

- In another pan, heat 1 tbsp oil and add the noodles and cook for 3 mins.

- For each serving bowl, add some noodles and top with a scoop of sauce and top with parmesan.

Serves: 6

Egg-Based Fettuccini Alfredo

Another alternative to regular noodles is to create egg-based 'noodles'.

Ingredients

- 2 eggs
- 28 g low fat cream cheese
- pinch of salt
- pinch of garlic powder
- ⅛ tsp black pepper

For the sauce:

- 28 g low fat sour cream
- 1 tbsp grated parmesan cheese
- 1 tbsp margarine

Directions

- In a food processor, blend the eggs, cheese, salt, garlic and pepper. Pour in a baking pan and bake at 200 degree Celsius for 8 mins. Let it cool, and then with a spatula remove the sheet of 'pasta'. Roll it up and slice it. Unroll it and place it aside.

- In a bowl, mix together the sauce ingredients and microwave for half a minute. Whisk again.

- Add the sauce to the pasta and toss to combine. Serve warm.

Serves: 2

Lentil Bolognese

Ingredients

- 96 grams lentils
- Extra-virgin olive oil
- 1 onion, chopped
- 1 stalk celery, chopped
- 1 carrots, chopped
- sea salt
- black pepper
- oregano
- 237 ml tomato sauce
- 59 ml vinegar
- 255 grams soba noodles
- parmesan cheese, grated

Directions

- Cook the lentils and the noodles according to the instructions on the package.

- In a pan, heat some oil and add the chopped vegetables, salt, pepper and oregano. Stir, cover and cook until golden.

- Next add the tomato sauce and cook for 5 mins. Add the vinegar and cook until it evaporates.

- Blend the lentils then add it to the pan and stir.

- Serve the noodles with the Bolognese sauce and sprinkle some parmesan on top.

Serves: 4

Vegetarian Involtini

Normal involtini, or braciola, is a sliced meat dish. This is a meatless alternative using eggplant. With a couple of ingredient swaps, you can turn this recipe vegan.

Ingredients

- 1 eggplant, trimmed, sliced
- kosher salt
- olive oil
- tomato sauce
- fat-free half and half
- Parmigiano, grated

Filling

- 100 g bread crumbs
- 100 g low fat milk ricotta
- Zest of 1 lemon
- Juice of 1/2 lemon
- 1 tsp. fresh thyme leaves, minced
- 1/4 tsp. kosher salt

Directions

- Sprinkle salt on the eggplant slices and place in the colander and rest for an hour. Press the moisture and pat them dry.

- In a deep saucepan, heat the oil and place the eggplants and cook for 3 mins. Transfer to a plate with paper towels to drain

- To make the filling just mix together all the ingredients and stir.

- Preheat the oven to 200 degree Celsius, in a baking dish, spoon the tomato sauce into the dish in a thin layer. Place a spoonful of the filling on one end of the eggplant slices and place it into the dish on top of the sauce. Spoon some cream on each rolls to moisten, and bake until the edges are golden for 25 mins.

- Garnish with parmigiano.

Serves: 2

Risotto Primavera

Ingredients

- 1 tbsp oil
- 1 onions, sliced
- 3 cloves garlic, crushed
- 150 grams zucchini, halved, sliced
- 100 grams green beans, cut in long pieces
- 100 grams broccoli, cut into florets
- 175 grams Arborio rice
- 800 ml vegetable stock
- 3 tbsp pine nuts
- 3 tbsp fresh parsley, chopped
- 4 tbsp extra-virgin olive oil

Directions

- In a large pan, heat the oil and add all the vegetables and cook for 5 mins. Transfer to a bowl and place aside.

- Add the rice to the pan and stir for a few minutes then slowly add the stock. Keep stirring and cook it over medium heat until the stock is absorbed and the rice is cooked.

- Blend together the parsley, pine nuts and oil to create a pesto sauce.

- Return the vegetables into the pan with the almost-cooked rice and add the pesto and season with salt and pepper and stir to combine.

- Serve warm and top with pine nuts and some pesto.

Swordfish with Olives

Ingredients

- 6 swordfish
- olive oil
- 6 cloves garlic, chopped
- 1 onions, chopped finely
- 1 celery heart, sliced
- 1 carrots, chopped
- 34 grams capers
- 20 green olives, pitted
- 118 ml white wine vinegar
- 37 grams raisins
- 5 leaves, chopped
- 45 grams pine nuts
- salt
- black pepper

Directions

- In a pan over medium heat, heat the oil and cook the fish just until the translucent flesh becomes milky, remove from the pan and set aside.

- In a separate large pan, cook the garlic, onion, celery, and carrot in olive oil until tender, add the capers, olives, vinegar, raisins, mint leaves, and pine nuts and cook for 4 mins. Adjust seasoning and return the fish, cover and cook. Taste and season with salt, if needed. Grind some pepper into it, as well. If the pan seems in danger of drying, add up to 1/2 cup of water. Return the fish to the pan, cover, cook for 5 more mins.

Serves: 6

Marco Polo Spaghetti

A healthy, alkalizing spaghetti recipe.

Ingredients

- 227 grams whole grain spaghetti
- 90 grams toasted pine nuts
- 118 ml black olives, chopped
- 70 grams roasted red peppers
- 15 grams parsley, chopped
- 11 grams fresh basil, chopped
- ground black pepper
- sea salt
- 1 tsp garlic, minced
- 4 tbsp olive oil
- Parmesan, grated

Directions

- Cook the spaghetti according to the instructions on the package. In a pan, toast the pine nuts until golden. In a bowl, combine the pine nuts, olives, peppers, herbs. Add some salt and pepper and mix.

- Heat the olive oil in a pan and add the garlic then add in the cooked spaghetti. Transfer to a serving platter and top with some of the nut mixture and sprinkle some parmesan on top.

Serves: 2

A Message from Andrea

Thank you so much for taking the time to read this book. I hope that this was of some benefit to you.

You can find many more books like this one I've created by checking out my Amazon page at the following address: http://www.amazon.com/Andrea-Silver/e/B00W820AR6/.

You can also get in touch with me personally at AndreaSilverWellness@gmail.com if you have any questions or ideas.

Made in the USA
Monee, IL
02 October 2025

31314099R00046